H.M.C.G.

A collection of poetry by Jessica Fisher

"Love is friendship set on fire." -Eric Jerome Dickey

The wildfire grew so suddenly, neither knew where the spark came from. Neither knew they had been ablaze all along...Heavy.

The Flames

We were friends
what happened?
one breath
one near-kiss
now air is on fire
between us
white-knuckling
a tortuous bliss
threatening an ecstasy
that will leave us
either dripping
or bleeding
will it save me?
or finish killing me?
I'm yearning but
I swear I'm dying
this raw, sudden passion
is suffocating me
meanwhile
I only hold you closer and tighter
urging you to keep squeezing
yoni threatening
to separate herself from me
to give herself to you
she's fearless
I fear you
I fear these mutinous feels
who've now
laid themselves bare before you
not sure what's happening here
or when these feelings got there
were you aware?
who put them there?
I'm totally fond of you
I love you
we were friends
what happened?
were you holding out on me?
or I on you?
are we both such scaredy cats

that we match
in both hoping the other
is just as attached?
will we speak on it?
never that
the jokes flow
to spare the awkward yearning
each flashback to that moment
leaves my soul burning
that moment
was everything I need
oh no
now I know
you need me
and I you
but what do we do?
we tiptoed that thin line between
fear and ecstasy
staring at our own desires
I'm staring at you
staring at me
but we're saying
and showing
nothing
no one is speaking
I'm suffering
he's still squeezing
Jesus help me
passion nearing overload
if it explodes
we're doomed souls
ascending a heaven
reserved for sinners
finding flames and pleasure
fearing neither hell nor the devil
I know nothing
only your heat penetrating mine
only my hands searching and squeezing
only my breath on your neck
in great, heaving breaths

that moment ten months pregnant
with our anticipation and suspense
I'll die if our lips
don't touch soon
I feel you
I'm squirming
there's no one here
to save us from ourselves
what happened?
in that split second
unbearable sparks between us
oh sweet jesus
just take me
but the alarm went off
the passion froze
a cold shower
and powerful imagination
is enough to convince us
this was just a dream
so we carry on
still floating
from a dream
we're both smiling
now in plain sight
I finally see you
I see you seeing me
possibly for the first time
I know what comes next
do you?
You're smiling
you know too
no more hiding, Your Highness
I knew you before
but now
i SEE you
we were friends
before that moment
what happened?
Nothing
Just a King finally finding his bravery
and a Queen finally embracing her royalty

Two Days Later

He is only a face
a voice, a presence, an embrace
a whisper in my right ear
a beautiful smile and eye contact
he is my favorite type
of worst nightmare
he is only a touch
a squeeze, a warmth
I feel him everywhere
he is what he does to me
hyper-awareness and sensitivity
heart palpitations and electricity
I light up when he touches me
hopes, dreams, desires, vulnerability
all awaken when he looks at me
I am looking at him
but staring at destiny
staring at where I want to be
staring at a lion, a protector, a provider
a powerhouse of gentle affection meets ferocity
an intoxicating blend of muscles and tattooed perfection
the deeper parts of me shiver to think
what type of lover he could be
I dare to dream about his agility and dexterity
with the female body, with my body, with me
I look at him and a tigress awakens in me
suddenly he is mine to protect and love
mine to quench his every desire
mine to uplift and submit to
yet mine to push, confront, and stand up to
when I need to
mine to comfort, nurture, and care for
mine to live and die for
I want him and all that comes with him
his good, his bad, his flaws, his sorrows
I want to be part of his better tomorrow
I want to kiss his imperfections into invisibility
when he gazes at a mirror
I want him to see what I see
it won't be perfection but

he'll see why he's perfect for me
his mistakes, his stumbles, his shortcomings
won't matter to me
I want to be the starting point
from which his growth accelerates exponentially
I want to be his better half
want him to be the better half of me
want him to know that love is blind
now two days later, I can't see

Night Light

Reveal all your fears
illuminate
fear the dark
even in light, hiding
seems backwards
if I'm hiding
it's the light I'd be shying
from
how come
you find security
in light
where everyone can see?
should not it be the darkness
you're craving?
makes for better hiding
if you don't want me to see
take the light from me
put it out
too scary?
no light, just you and me
it's dark, you have to feel me
are you staring?
what do you see?
nothing?
precisely
FEEL ME
feel my passion, my pain
I feel you yearning, feeling the same
I feel your conscience deciding
challenging or hiding
fighting or flighting
but in the meantime
fears forgotten
your lips on mine
darkness surrounds us
I taste you smiling
heartbeat racing
you're running
but not hiding

scared, but smiling
the passion is true
is that what scares you?
once darkness surrounds us two
there's no night light that can save you
you feel it
I do too
fight or flight
flee
or let it consume you

Threes and Six

Why does he matter
a question better
what's the matter

How did this happen
camera flashing
what's the caption

don't know what this is
can it be trusted
I'm suspicious

a song in my heart
stalling, false start
cracked, fell apart

savor the moment
temptation moaning
it's an omen

dreaming, don't pinch me
yet intriguingly
you terrify me

Le'Sigh

the accent follows me to my dreams
hauntingly enticing me
that sound is edible
it tastes so sweet
could I eat the words you speak
I'd soon grow fat from my greed
it feeds me on a level
where even food and religion cannot nourish me
it opens me up so my soul spills forth
but your path is the roughest course
and loving me is anything but easy
I tell myself repeatedly, you aren't for me
but when you're looking down at me
I swear I see destiny
any day that has you in it is instantly happy
always happy to see you, even when I'm angry
even when I cuss and scream
I still want you near me
knowing you don't feel the same
doesn't change a thing
my feelings have no contingencies
my anger is fueled by passion
it burns angry hot and icy blue
what's more, it completely engulfs you
until we are tangled in angry ecstasy
sweating...breathing heavily
as you whisper that it belongs to me
I tell myself repeatedly, you are not for me
but really, I've put my name on you
it's why you cannot explain sudden needs
to sleep beside me, just to be near me
it's why you squeeze so tightly
even in sleep, always touching me
so tell me repeatedly that you like your freedom
I'll tell you repeatedly that's not what I'm after
however
remember the fire I stir in your loins
remember my touch, my kiss, my lips
remember my lips and legs wrapped around you

remember how your climaxes cripple you
and the groans that escape you when I bite you
remember how your body ignites when I touch you
remember my naked body, how it feels pressed against you
remember my thighs and the curve of my behind
then remember, you so cherished your freedom
that eventually
these memories will be all you have left of me
after this affair dies with the season
I'll remember the man and the accent
that I loved for no good reason
I have no reason
no answer for why I loved you
I never chose to

Excuse my English

It's French
I couldn't catch the accent
he told me he loved me...in French
but he seemed so angry
for all I know
he's leaving me
why else would a single tear
gather, then disappear
why would a single drop of sorrow
show itself, and then retract
the sight only mine to borrow
a sight I wasn't supposed to behold
retracted like a secret almost told
I look into those dreamy eyes
and cannot tell where his affections lie
he seems so angry
what is he saying?
It's French
his eyes
is that a look of despise
or is he terrified?
is he leaving...or pleading?
I'm frustrated, I scream
JUST TELL ME
and he does
with a kiss stolen from the bliss
found only in my wildest dreams
it's not hatred burning for me
it's passion, burning vehemently
he kisses me like he means to keep me
from leaving
is that what he thinks is happening?
is he trying to save me from lonely?
I need him to....desperately
my english words won't be swerved
can't form the pronunciation and proper accent
necessary to make it meaningful in French
his pleading eyes are heavy
he hears me speaking, knows not what I'm saying

he can't understand, his heart is breaking
as I tell him a world without him
isn't a life worth living
I'm pleading now, sobbing
please don't leave me
he is sobbing with me
saying he loves me, needs me
I don't understand what he's saying
my heart is breaking
eyes heavy with pain, he turns away
so that's it...suddenly I can't breathe
my heart shatters immediately
then, as if he heard my heart breaking
he's back in front of me
one tear on his face, smiling

Frenchy's Watching

I'm watching him read
it's Frenchy
he's reading "Excuse my English"
right in front of me
I know he's wondering
if he was there
while I was dreaming
the answer is no
the dream that inspired that poetry
did not involve Frenchy...directly
he cannot tell the creativity from reality
did I blur the lines enough to hide
safely behind my veil of mystery?
he finished it, he's smiling
I cannot say why
I don't know what he's thinking
it's unnerving
I feel him watching me
he's done, but I'm still scribbling
I cannot help smiling
I feel him, feeling for me
he's searching my face
the question is lingering
now I'm smiling
what I'm not doing
is answering
He calls me
his voice softly
urging me
my delicate defiance
defines me
I'm still writing
still smiling
not answering
I don't know what he wants from me
I have to go
he's calling me
Jay's considering
Frenchy's watching

Salsa Guy

He hates me
this is no laughing matter
it's not an act
he JUST met me
a second ago
I think he means it
except he's smiling
amidst his gleaming smile
I see something else shining
I mean, he's REALLY smiling
showing all teeth, utterly pleased
he's speaking, saying
'you have to get away from me"
but he's still touching me, leading me
we're still dancing
I follow him through this song
and into the next, it feels so right
so right, I'm sure to
follow him to his dreams tonight
no, it's okay, hold on to me
unless you're afraid to bare your soul
because I want to see
I promise you, I will look
if you let me close enough
me llamo Jessica
soy la noche
you are night seeker
I take your hand
I feel the connection
see the pain
goodbye song, goodbye night
I left not knowing his name
that dance never left me
I never was the same

Nekkid

If you could hear it, would it make a sound?
Would you be able to hear my delicate round browns
or just the sound of my see-through undergarments slowly sliding down?
If we were on opposite sides of a pitch-black room
and I undressed and walked over to you
by the time i reached you, you'd prolly be naked too
Why?
Because my nudity would grip you, and you'd catch it like the flu
I don't care what you say, your all-time favorite color is butt-naked-brown
or, at least it will be once these lights go down
but first, leave the lights on
There's so much I want to do to you, so much I want you to see me do
I love the skin I was born in, and even more than I'm proud of it
I want you to take a dive in it
The motion in my ocean is flowing
but understand there's more to sailing a ship than just the size of it
without the nautical sense to navigate it, you may not be able to handle it
the waters will be rough and if you capsize prematurely, the tide will surely be missed
I want you to role play a little bit
I'll be the sexy little love boat keeping you afloat
meanwhile, you put on your sailor's cap, thrust your back, and stroke
truth be told, I can sail my own ship, however
I want you to be the tropical storm that rocks it
or better yet, on a wave of emotion, pull out your surfboard and ride it
Or, we could always stay ashore
Besides, I've been dying to try what Ne-yo had in mind
except, let's do it in a house of mirrors so I can see from every angle and every side
I want you to witness the epitome of ebony essence
with just the right touch of excess in the places that accentuate me best
With all of this optical aphrodisiac, there will be no need for tequila or cognac
I want you to witness me in my most vulnerable state
once the lights go out, all visual perceptions will go to waste
I want you to watch me wide-eyed as I swerve my hips, thighs, and voluptuous behind
as R-Kelly begins to play, transforming me into the poster child for slow wind
I want you to watch me wind and grind, wearing nothing but cologne
but please try to focus on me as all your bodily fluids flee
and take sanctuary in your love-making zone
Apparently the naked truth was better than you could have ever fathomed
I watched in awe as you suffered from the first every eye-gasm

I'm standing there, completely bare
wetter than a rainstorm in open seas, nude as the winter trees
my body hot and scorching, even though the thermometer reads a normal 98.6 degrees
I'm so hot I'm exhaling steam
as we approach zero degrees of separation, or absolute proximity
I want you to feel no self-doubt
lay your head back, relax, let this whipped cream and I end your drought
let my moisture replenish you, but first,
turn the lights out

An entry from my journal: 10/3/2017

"Love: Giving a damn about someone, even against your will and better judgement"
    -Jessica Fisher

I don't believe in love. A good friend and somewhat of a spirit guide of mine asked me (challenged me rather) to redefine love in a way that I found acceptable and, for lack of a better word, believable. This quote was my reply the following day. It made him laugh. It wasn't merely a chuckle, he laughed a deep, throaty laugh that came from his gut and made him throw his head back...all in sheer amazement and entertainment. I don't know that he's ever met anyone with such a strong defiant streak against something so inevitable and powerful. However, I challenge the notion that love conquers all. I challenge love to allow you to keep your wits once it has consumed you. I challenge love to be accomplished without giving reasons to be unintelligent and irrational. Love = overstimulation. It's not actually pleasant. We're told it's supposed to be that way, but says who? For something that no one has ever done right, why does everyone think they're an expert? The key to loving successfully lies in not falling in love in the first place. Love isn't some chance thing that happens to you. It can be a conscious, intentional, intelligent decision. It's only irrational because we're irrational, and we're irrational because we're human and our brains are so smart they fooled themselves into thinking that they are, in fact, rational. We are hopelessly human. I'm stating all of this so that my next human knows that I will not be ruled by my heart's radical emotions nor my brain's radical irrationality.

The Hi Reply

I just want you to know
that not so very long ago
a simple poem to tell me hi
made me smile, made me sigh
that simple rhyme
got stuck in my head
now thoughts of you
follow me to bed

Twin Flame

hello gemelo
how did I not recognize you
I've been mirroring you
gemelo mio
candela gemelo de mio
I have been missing
and not knowing
that I've been needing
you
was all of that empty
me feeling you
missing and not knowing
me?
sweet jeezus
you're telling me you could feel me
missing, subconsciously reaching
on the surface, strangers
bonding suddenly
quickly and unexplainably
hello gemelo mio
te extraño
I just met you
nice to meet you
and already love you before
candela gemelo mio
mi amor

Every Vein

I imagined coming home everyday to you
I imagined jumping the broom with you
I imagined being married to you
I imagined the things I'd do to you
and for you, on our honeymoon
I imagined taking belly and pole dancing
so I could strip and perform for you
I imagined coming second only
to the daughter I wanted to give you
I imagined watching your fatherhood bloom
imagined Sidney's face being
a perfect mixture of me and you
I imagined my love only magnifying for you
as trials and tribulations only brought
me closer to you
I imagined being 75, in my rocking chair
on my porch, rocking next to you
and if death found you first, I imagined
my death would soon follow suit
because I couldn't imagine living without you
I imagined the coroner finding your name
tattooed on my heart and in every vein
I imagined the reason for my code blue
the conclusion of my autopsy
my cause of death simply being
no more you

The Mapmaker

What is it about you? Maybe it's the succulent traces of your lips, or the gentle aggression of your kiss. A kiss that never touched my lips, but made me believe that bliss did exist. You are my priceless, over-appreciated gift, the gift that should have touched my lips. If not that, it must be the warm penetrance of your gaze that warms my desires and sets my self-sexiness ablaze, like you could have any donut you wish, but it's my glaze you crave. What I'd give for that warm penetrance, I want to feel the haze. I want to feel it start at the earlobe, and take a long, slow road trip south. But what good's a road trip if you don't make a few stops? Stop at the nape and nibble a bit. I want you to bother my tectonic plates and cause an erotic earthquake. Don't be alarmed if you feel my palm run down your thighs as my tides begin to rise. Just as the moon arouses the ocean, you finely tune my body with circular tongue motions, and get my ocean's river flowing. Don't fight with the current, roll with the flow. Let your instincts discern where I want you to go. Navigate your senses and they'll point you in the right direction. Look, listen, smell, and most importantly, touch and taste your way through every hill, valley, dip, crevice, and curve your survey as you explore terrain de Jay. From the ends of my earlobes, to the tips of my toes, after this trip there should be no part of me that your mouth doesn't know. After all that oral exploration, so pleased that I was almost aching, my body was so exhausted with sensation that my face was left vacant. After a slight pause and a moment of ocular fixation, I thought you were done, but you had just begun. You recited a poem and let me forget that there's always a punchline at the end of a rhyme. So with nowhere left to roam, you accelerated north and *AHEM* drove your point home. I was already feeling the rhyme, but the punchline was so breathtaking I almost died. Bent over backwards with passion and ecstasy, for hours you entertained me with feats of endurance and flexibility. Then suddenly it hit me that all along you knew how bad I had longed for you to run all along and through my erogenous zones. But by this time, the deed was through and my frontier had been named after you. A final unrelenting glance at the chandelier, and that painful bliss that I thought didn't exist was clear, and expressed as a flash-flood and a tear.

Unhinged

Overwhelmed by you and everything you say and do
your voice unhinges me, yet I'm stuck to you
where's the glue? No need
already stuck to you, Latched
Sam Smith, Disclosure'd to you
I'm pages in a new book to you
white on rice in the snow on you
I'm hair glue on a piece of weave
I'm on you like a wig on Annalise Keating
you are both my lover and president
I'm Liv, you're both Jake and Fitz
we go together like salad and bacon bits
fat kids and cake, chips and dip
We go together like Elsa and ice
but i'm not letting go, quite frankly
I hope this blizzard stays
"The cold never bothered me anyway"

When Jay Has A Crush

When Jay has a crush, nobody knows which way is up
lol, jk, nobody even knows
not even the crush
actually he's the last to know
if the feels even last long enough to tell him so
She doesn't fall for people…..easily
that's a lie, she falls without warning...suddenly
the battle to get from bristling with defiance
to openly gushing, bruh
iss tedious and soul crushing
on the inside she's only fighting herself
self-inflicting hope and helplessness
all in the same breath
cursing his name for bringing this stress
she's under her own duress
she'll fight and plead with her feelings
but he's her twin flame
no matter how much that leaves her reeling
the bottom line is something inside of her
sees herself in him, their energies already married
a little fish reeling on the bottom line, the irony
isn't lost on her, nor does she find it funny
Funny isn't it
she spends all her time laughing
not realizing she's falling
not realizing the flames are reaching
his heart is calling
she defies her ears to deaf
while she catches her breath
no, this can't be happening
little fish is reeling, and falling
meanwhile, he's waiting patiently
ironically, this time he was the first to know
when my heart flutters, he feels the echos
he smiles at me knowingly
amusedly watching my eyes rolling
as I make a final defiant stand
then turn to putty in his hands
damn, here we go for the first time, again

Stranger Danger

I don't know when he first saw me
don't know how long he's been watching me
I didn't know I was his beauty
could have bumped me in the crowded street
didn't notice him turn and follow me
he doesn't care that I know he's admiring
he brought it to my attention
he's bold
now I'm paranoid
I know he'll come for me eventually
he told me
he talks with me, but he won't touch me
I'm his small piece of gold with diamond eyes
too priceless to touch, too alluring to leave
he's guarding me
his precious jewelry
I don't know him, he barely knows me
that's about to change
because now he knows I know he's watching
he knows where to find me, he makes me nervous
he keeps me looking over my shoulder
for a face I've never laid eyes on
I don't know his face
I know his voice
it smulders, it's hot lava descending slowly
it burns right through me
gives me chills, freezes me where I stand
my goosebumps the only exception
it rings in my head at night, it hinders my sleep
sometimes I dream he's right behind me
saying nothing, only breathing
sometimes the dream seems so real
I almost feel his breath on me
I almost feel his weight beside me
almost feel his fingertips tracing my spine
makes me shudder, I'm terrified
I'm paralyzed
I don't realize it's only a dream
I lay there helplessly

trembling, shaking, cowering, doing everything
to keep myself from screaming
then I jerk awake, I'm alone, sweating
no, he has never touched me
but he knows me intimately
he has never laid a finger
yet somehow, he's inside me
my every thought, every fear, every fantasy
he knows that I'm hiding
he doesn't know, I hope he finds me
the suspense, such a sweet anxiety
I hope he's stalking me
If I'm the most beautiful thing he's ever seen
why not kidnap me?
I promise I won't scream
then it happened, he caught me
I'm afraid of him, but he's just staring
he's savoring the proximity, basking in
the essence of me
he's imagining caressing me, touching lightly
massaging gently, nuzzling and cuddling
he's imagining himself wrapped lovingly around me
he's imagining my face laying next to his
imagining that I'm his Queen
what he can't imagine
is why I would think
that he would ever hurt me
secretly, he loves me
he wants to steal from me
my sorrows, pains, trials, my tears
he wants to empower me
to replace my melancholy with happy
so he tortures me
with acute passion, affection, joy, and pleasure
he threatens to make it a chronic condition
he scares me, because he chose me
he won't rest until he makes me happy
he caught me
but I'm not tied or bound to anything
I'm free to leave
he has a hold on me
my fear is giving way to yearning
shivering still, now from anticipation

my breathing is unsteady
heart is skipping beats
my cheeks are flushing
I may die if he doesn't touch me
he told me I can leave
but I'm panicking
begging for the torture to proceed
I refuse to leave
I need him, need his touch, his love
until I get it, I won't budge
he knows me intimately, I know him barely
I know I'm falling, don't catch me
he's dangerous, I'm throwing caution to the wind
He is a stranger
I fell for him

Dreams Talking To Me

My Queen, I am ready
I know you do not believe me
but I will not sleep peacefully
until you belong to me
you don't believe it's true
but everyday I'll prove to you
why I deserve you
because you, my Queen
have suffered long enough already
you are more than enough, for me
my Queen
I am fighting for you
won't rest until I prove to you
that I am your King
I love you
I know you still don't believe me
that's fine with me
but hear this Queen
I. Am. Ready.
your fear does not scare me
neither does loving you
my only fear now
is living a life without you
Your Highness
forgive me, but
I don't need your permission
to make you love me
if a hostile takeover is needed
so be it
dammit!
my Queen
I'm sorry I'm just a dream

Fearless & Fragile

Fearless: I stare recklessly into your eyes, daring you to push me

Fearless: I am daringly defiant, demanding you to chase me

Fearless: You are not mine, but your aura, your energy, belongs to me

Fearless: You are you, I am me, and we are we, but freely

Fearless: I belong to no one but me, but I am more yours than anybody's

Fragile: I feel desolately weak, needing only your arms around me

Fragile: I need and need and need, sometimes resolving to cowardice & hiding

Fragile: Your embrace compresses the pieces, fixing nothing, but holding them together

Fragile: I would be falling apart, were you not holding me together

Fragile: You are the rock supporting me comfortingly, while I put myself back together

Fearless: I don't need you

Fragile: But I do

Fearless: You are free

Fragile: Can I keep you

Fearless: You don't need me

Fearless: I can live without you

Fragile: I hope you want me

Fragile: I don't want to

Fearless: Here I am

Fragile: Will you keep me?

Fearless: I am broken

Fragile: Will you save me?

Fearless: I love me more than I love you

Fragile: Loving me is how I know I love you

Fearless: I am fragile, but I am sure of you

Fragile: I am fearless, except when it comes to you

Dream 12/22

I had a dream
Rishi was talking
We were partnering
Everyone already thinks we're sleeping
together, so whatever
let's fuel the fire
You're in the center
fighting for your feels to not bust through
deja vu
I'm searching your face and seeing you yearning
but instead of staying in place
I go to you
I'm standing in front of you, my hands on your waist
making eye contact with you
seven seconds later, I'm whispering to you
"Your Highness,
I love you, I see you
It's not a love you can get rid of or ruin
no matter what you do, I love you
beyond my control or yours
there's nothing you can do to ruin or spoil
the affections I have for you
whoever you are, and whoever you become
this place you have in my heart will always bear your name
If life sends us our separate ways, my love will stay the same
if the universe sends us to each other, to love each other in a romantic capacity
still, my love will stay the same
it's a love without conditions or expectations
my love for you doesn't depend on what you feel for me
it comes with no sense of entitlement or possession
I love you like I love a wild thing
like a free and feral bird I love, but cannot contain
because to take away your freedom would crush my heart
because to see you any other way than free and happy
would be the end of me
so no, my love does not mean I have the right to keep you
It just means I love you
no matter who you are or what you do
no matter what you do with who

my connection to you is like my connection to nature
inescapable. inevitable.
my love for you is non-debatable
and just because I don't think you heard me
there is nothing you can do
to stop my love for you
all I need, is for you to just
be you
the freedom of your spirit
is the most alluring thing about you
who am I to take that from you
don't let anyone touch that part of you
it is sacred and forbidden
it comes before everything
it is the core of your essence and my attraction
it is the heartbeat behind why I love you
and why my love will NEVER involve shackles or glue
we belong to each other
the way the birds and the bees belong to the trees
we belong to each other
freely
I am your Queen, I adore you
and I do so only because I damn well please
there's nothing you can do, to stop me"
my whispered speech ends there, I simply hug you
I feel the tears on my cheeks, but I know
I need to just hold you
everything fades to black except us two
we stay attached at the hip for the remainder of the weekender
and when the time came to catch our planes
you held on a little tighter, for a little longer
the eye contact lasted, and ended in a long forehead kiss
followed by another embrace, this one even longer
the energy in that embrace told me everything
The embrace was a prequel to a kiss, this is what woke me…
my heart is racing, what's happening?
The dream was a dream
the speech is still sitting with me, and now that I've written it down
it's technically tantigle reality, the feels felt so real, I'm wondering
if my subconscious is trying to tell me that it's finally time to tell you
that dream was a deja vu re-do, except this time, it showed me feels I kept from you
I didn't know until the dream spelled it out for me
It's you…you are what's happening to me. It's not a dream.

Mr. Write

Dear Mr. Write
Mister W-R-I-T-E
You don't have to be right for me
R-I-G-H-T
To be my Mr. Write-For-Me
W-R-I-T-E
Written expressions are to me
What a gold digger thinks of fine jewelery
I crave something more than money
I crave vocabulary, I crave verbal intimacy
Mr. Write, Mr. Write
Make every word touch me
Caress me articulately
Verbalize me softly
Strum my pain with spoken words
Let your voice carry the waves of
Mental stimulation all over me
Penetrate me
With your epiphanies and deeper thinking
Mr. Write, Mr. Write
Go deep as you can
Go until bliss breaches near pain
Recite until bliss and pain
Make love and leave me in blain
Mr. Write, Mr. Write
How your prose pursues me
It follows me to my dreams
It's contradictory it seems
It's a sweet, well-known mystery
That follows closely, yet still eludes me
It seems to torture me
As much as it pleases me
Mr. Write say things I haven't heard already
By not speaking and resolving to show me
How your world doesn't revolve without me
Mr. Write, Mr. Write
I'm naturally distrusting
Don't count on me listening
Unless you're willing to

Write everything in bold
Scribe it legibly so I can see clearly
Then act it out, perform it for me
Perform it so the world can see
I don't trust anything
That must be done in secrecy
Love is a robust verb
And cannot be done discreetly
Enunciate proudly that
You need me through a refusal
To live without me
Not through a vague and vain necessity
Stress every syllable to me
Whisper to me your rhymes and theories
Allow them to tickle my fancy
Accentuate perfectly, then repeat
Repeatedly until the rhythm
And verbal idiosyncrasies
Ravage me to near lunacy
Mr. Write, Mr. Write
Recite for me
Let each poetic verse
Sing a song for me
Sing a song, sing it soft
Sing it long for me
Sing until Mr. Write is so right
He feels almost wrong to be so right
For me
Pronounce your lyrical genius
Spell it out for me
Put it on display to appease me
Offer it like one offers dowery
Command the vocabulary
Make it bow before me
Mr. Write, Mr. Write
Make me your Queen
Pledge your allegiance, your pen, your paper
To me and all my royalty
Let them be your shield and sword
Take up your arms, fight for me
Claim your victory, then
Let me honor your bravery
Kneel before me, Mr. Write

Arise Sir Write, my new Black Knight
K-N-I-G-H-T
Arise my Knight, drop the H-T
Arrange the letters remaining
to rhyme with sing
Arise Mr. Write
My K-I-N-G
Mr. Right-Beside-Me
Mr. Go-To-The-End-Of-Earth-For-Me
He's not Mr. Perfect
He's Mr. Right-for-me
R-I-G-H-T

The Journal entry attached to this poem: dated 3/5/17

"I don't remember writing this poem (I wrote it back in May of 2012). Cannot remember who or what the inspiration was. It seems like I'm reaching out to someone in particular, specifically. Since this is one I never shared, they surely know nothing of what I was apparently asking. Who the hell was I talking to?? I'm sure it doesn't matter now. Whoever the poor soul was, he probably dodged a bullet. The 2012 me needed serious therapy. The mom issues and trust issues (possibly one and the same) ruled everything I thought I knew. He would not have stood a chance back then. I just wanted someone to write to me. Write something to and for me. I wanted love letters and rhyming poetry. I wanted him to cherish me verbally. Like I said, I don't recall any of the deets about who, real or imagined, I wanted this from. Perhaps it was a cry out to the universe to send him to me. I let Megs read this and she raved, said it was one of her favs. I trust her judgement, so it's highly likely that now it's a secret to nobody. Just in case he's reading this, write me love letters and poetry. Send me flower-shaped fruit and candy. Shower me with overt affection, make me feel important. Save me...Moment.

House of Pain

This is my house now
I kissed the front door on my way in
I can feel the pulse of this house screaming
for some semblance of someone remotely worthy
of holding the key
This house of flames is inflamed and untamed
I find it cozy…
There's cuddly teddy bears and deadly polar bears
juicy secrets, comfy sweats, endless ammo, and silencers
also, strangely, a sign on the screen that says
'Great Rising Young Queen'
punctuated with a crown and black heart emoji
and also strangely, a tiny picture of highschool me
Intriguing....
You saw me coming
you saw me, even back then
small, bookish, quiet, shy
words and smiles reserved only for my friends
A quiet storm who paced the halls
quietly praying for invisibility, I made an art of blending in
and you, only barely a man but just as tall
athletic, popular, handsome...you captivated them all
everyone clamoring to befriend you
the athletes envious, wanting to be you
the girls giggling and crushing on you
and then there was me, I never so much as made eye contact with you
You never said a word to me
but a tiny mental picture was made
and placed in a flame-retardant frame
For years I've been in here...simmering
My face decorated this house of pain
long before I knew you even knew my name
Now here I stand amidst the flames
Staring at my own face on the wall
as I tattoo the walls with my name
You see me

A flame moved and swayed by the waves
You, a tsunami, entranced by the dancing flames
This is a dance and a duel
All your methods are battle-tested
None of them can save you
I'm battle-tested too
This house is better at nothing else
than protecting itself
I'm no threat to your security
yet secretly, you've been low-key doing recon on me
secretly admiring and pondering
contemplating every facial expression
every inflection of my mole
as the healthy skepticism
with a subtle air of royalty
sends my eyebrow aloof
with amused, dubious curiosity
I see you too
This castle is you
The flames are everything
life tried to do to you to break you
strong, steadfast, determined, deadly
wise, ambitious, passionate, you are personified royalty
The flames unleashed a fiery hell
and still they failed to destroy you
most curiously,
the flames seemed to nurture you
From the ashes was born a man
where a troubled boy used to stand
You crowned yourself King of legendary resilience and loyalty
I see you, Your Highness
The Phoenix King
Forever may you reign
Supreme ruler of these flames
These chaotic flames are alive and breathing
I hear them whispering sweetly
beckoning soothingly
softly chanting my name
Queen Jay, forever may she reign
Queen Jay, forever may she reign
This is my house now

Sage and Ancestors Saved You

The sage is burning
And I'm meditating
The kitten is mewing and playing
I suspect she feels the turbulence
Rustling just beneath my skin
and tho the raging GODDESS has the boat rocking and swaying
I feel the compression of my volatile emotions within
The kitten blinks slowly and continues purring
The sage continues burning
The Goddess continues raging
But I cannot focus my mind on meditation
Four flames and one salt lamp
The 4 elements and my attitude
At least, let the white man tell it
My only feelings are what THEY project onto me
Ask me about my feelings
Then defensively belittle my perspective
THAT YOU ASKED FOR
then insert your own naive & assumptive projections
"Because other people have it like that too"
"Maybe it's just you…"
…..
You're one of those 'All lives matter" types
The type that openly worships the black goddess and her body
But also a MAGA Fox News digesting sheep
Your privilege precedes you
It's funny, I understand that you don't understand
But it's not my job to educate you.
And if I'm feeling gracious and want to help you understand
Don't spit in my face with your ignorant passive, presumptive racism that you still think is okay
Because you don't use the N word
And think black women are the shit
Which…we are, but I digress
Why does your dick get so hard for us
But your resolve to understand us is as flaccid
As your limp excuses for why you think it's ok
To tell a black women that her experiences
And her fears

And her perspective
And her knowledge
And her traumas
Aren't legitimate because hey,
Other people have it bad too...
No, FUHK YOU!
You've lived your privileged little life
In a privileged little bubble
Obsessed with your privileged little history books
That white washed all the blood and greed and genocide from the story....
Do not project hate into this piece because there isn't any
It's a little heated and angry
But I get it...
I understand why we no longer waste our breath trying to tell our story
I don't have the energy
So for that reason, the sage is burning
I've taken my noble seat to breathe
*****deep inhale*****deep exhale*****
But my pen is still angry
The meditation isn't happening
The kitten is still purring
The Goddess is still raging
The sage is still burning......
Because my ancestors are screaming
YOU DON'T WANT THIS SMOKE
And I don't want to openly flame you.......
....
So the sage is burning
My pen is simmering
The Goddess is calming
My mind is meditation ready
I am nobly seated and breathing
Thank MY ancestors tonight before you sleep
They are the only thing that saved you.

So this next one...I wasn't planning to release this piece until my next collection (wink), however something inside is screaming to include it (and some of the others I was saving for the next round) in this collection, even though it's a little out of place with what I was attempting to do with this collection. So, in the grandest spirit of 'I do what I want', I'm dropping this bomb. It's a significant piece for me because the subject matter is one that I could not bring myself to share for a very long time. Anyone who knows me, knows my ex is a human I mention but never really talk about in depth. He has inspired exactly three poems ever, this one, one you've already read if you made it this far, and another you have yet to read somewhere in the following pages. I have what I have lovingly named 'big bang poetry', and it's only born of explosive emotions big enough to collapse the sun. It's only then that I am able to create something. Well, to put it more correctly, it's only then that these pieces force themselves out of me. There is no human walking this earth that has inspired more poetry out of me than Frenchy. This following piece however, erupted from me like an angry fire baby 5 years overdue from a hostile flame-retardant womb down a stenotic birth canal. This piece was a figurative bullet. I felt my chakras vibrating once my pen stopped discharging. The shot was taken long ago, this poem is the shell casing finally dropping...Crush.

I Am Untitled #7

I remember the bar, I remember the line
I remember thinking, 'Dammit, a 4th time'
I was not her, he was relieved
mistaken identity, truth? or an excuse to talk to me?
but he was a cutie, meh, I let him slide
he smiled a timid smile that never reached his eyes
when I gave him my number, I think he was surprised
shit, so was I…..whatevs, he's cute
what's the worst he could do?…..

My eyes are swollen and leaking, I'm not eating
breakfast and lunch were nausea and iced coffee
the world was gray and fuzzy
I autopilot my days, cried myself to sleep
I smiled to keep from shattering
I remember hunger pains and rain
but once food was in front of me, it disgusted me
an eerie metaphor for how I felt
a realization of how much damage I'd been blindly undertaking
when did I hand him my dimmer switch?
why didn't I notice my light slowly leaving me?
blindly at the hands of an autobot avataring as my Knight of Light
I watched the man I loved transform, his true form
a sinister robotic being, less man, more machine
He is DeceptiShawn

We were supposed to hit the bar
we spent it in his kitchen instead, sipping & rapping Nas lyrics
I left him reeling as I got lost in Nas's "One Mic", spitting every lyric perfectly
neither of us tipsy, both high off the chemistry
his kiss surprised me, both timid and earnest
shy, soft, firm, pleading, 'Jay will you love me?'
hanging in the post-kiss atmosphere
his smile finally touched his eyes, the boy inside the man was clear
him: 'where have you been all my life?'
me grinning and silly: 'right here'
beautiful apartment, very welcoming, very polite, very handsome
both gallant & goofy, confident & loving, ambitious & handworking
family-centered & god-fearing, I felt the universe bragging

when she placed him before me, but still, I had to choose
what do I have to lose?.....

It's been a week
my clothes loosely hug or hang from me
I'm drowning
each day feels like a year, nothing is clear
there's darkness and a fuzzy disassociation, far surpassing anything
the great Wall depression ever threw at me
I'm staring at the floor, seeing my own heart there, beating and bleeding
I make no move to rescue it
instead, I stare curiously, loosely wondering how long it will continue lasting
in this current state of being...will it stop? can it keep beating without me?
the jury is still out, I'm unreachable
coughing up water from my own salty tears
I want the sorrow to swallow me, yet I'm fighting to keep floating, keep breathing
everything is hardening, something's come loose
the walls are freezing around me
on the floor where my heart lay previously bleeding
there's now an unthawing iceberg, tears evaporate on my face
as tears are replaced with streaks of smoke, fire, and rage
The Phoenix flames the fires inside, my exterior an unbothered Ice Queen
I am the dragon reborn from the Ice King
I breathe & exhale frozen fire, laying waste to the shell of a woman that once was me
I am DeceptiShawn's final reckoning

I'm spending more nights at his place than mine
I remember bringing Leroy over the first time
I took pictures of him putting on his little coat, walking my little doggy for me
I listened to him laugh as I told stories about how bougie this little dog can be
we took pictures of Leroy in front of our first christmas tree
we watched "A Christmas Story" & baked cookies
I didn't tell my friends because I didn't want to jinx it
I mentioned my boyfriend in passing...everyone stopped...wait, WHAT?!
they all screamed & I died laughing, such a scene
they all couldn't wait to meet 'the man', they were happy for me
Brit and the Wallace made sure he knew what his fate would be if he hurt me
'iont want no shit outta you'....lol now it's official
Jay has a man, well damn.....

I snicker menacingly, fuhk his feelings
fuhk everything, I'm leaving
fuhk society's notions of love and believing

today, I do whatever the fuhk I want
I have neither a fuhk to lend or lean on where he's concerned
i am all frostbite or inferno
lava and lightning
deep space and absolute zero
I bounce fluidly and effortlessly between the extremes
with little to no in-between
what you think you see is a mirage, a deceptive mirror
I give up nothing, cleverly regurging what I see before me
I listen with a raised eyebrow as he empties his heart
he's crying, I'm silently contemplating buying groceries
hmm, I'm really craving a pop-tart
I'm an empath, but I tied that bitch up, gagged her with her own fuhking feelings
she's back in the far recesses of my brain crying
I am a tornado in an ice storm, with a wildfire at the eye
I flash my brightest, most sinister smile
Hi, I don't think we've met…

We are moving in together
he goes from zero to 2 pets instantly, he's absolutely delighted
sharing space, shopping, laughing, & roasting each other constantly
his mom is an absolute angel, we chat with her nightly
she's everything I would have wanted my mother to be
we're discussing meeting each other's families
sides hurting as we compare 'my family is crazy' stories
he took me to Tampa, I took him to Slower Lower Delaware
my first time bringing a man home to officially meet the Papa Bear
I think this could be the guy; poor guy
my family gathered, gaped, and swarmed him
I had never brought anyone home so they were dying to meet him
I even let him meet her, the female parental unit
this just might be it
fleeting thoughts of joining families swimming lazily around my dreams…..

I'm standing outside of myself, watching myself mirror feelings I can't reach or feel
I'm outside of me, watching me curiously, people falling in love with me
without me
how intriguing
I give nothing, they imagine their feelings then project them onto me
this is irrational as hell; did love make me this crazy?
why does anyone want this? why's he still harping on this?
didn't he decide this? didn't his insecurities deafen him and silence me?
his jury preemptively passed judgement, long before confronting me

didn't you stop touching me and start accusing me of cheating?
didn't you want me to leave? Didn't I almost need the cops to get my things?
why TF would I want that back?
the love I have left for him is a ghost; unreachable and intangible
he is nobody
I wouldn't touch that toxic love if it were standing right beside me

He brought a house, I lost my job; we made it work
the love continued only…
he never wants to go anywhere or do anything
we went dancing and bowling and each time
he accused me of eye fuhking somebody; are you kidding me?
oh it's the trust issues, he's contrite and sorry and vow to try harder
I give him the benefit of the doubt, I have them too
it's not easy, but was he blind to me waking up everyday and choosing him?
I warned him
If he didn't talk to me, his insecurities would speak louder than me
everything will disintegrate, he'll speak up, but be too late
Does he trust me? or has his insecurities already gagged me?.....

The bedroom is an arctic wasteland; the hardware won't stay hard
I sleep naked and can't sleep because he won't touch me
soon, his flaccidity is seeping into my feelings
now floppy & unfeeling, I think of my panic button, my Frenchy
I miss my friends, all of the ones he became 'uncomfortable' with
because they had penises
yet it was cool for him to chat with ex girlfriends
and express regrets about it not working with them
did he forget I was standing in the same fuhking room? I heard him
but he's checking my messages and call histories because 'I'm sneaky'
I'm paying for his ex's mistakes; she played him, then left him for her ex-dude
same one she cheated on him with
same one he felt entitled to talk to due to the 'captain save em' hard-on he still clings to
he still has it, she's still using him
he had passwords and codes, he saw everything, and still
it never settled his insecurities; regardless of finding nothing
but I'm sneaky and shady and untrustworthy
he told his bestie he keeps one eye open when asked if he trusted me
I line up a weekend with the girls and Isaiah, I need a weekend sanctuary…..

Frenchy is my enigma, my invisible ever-present muse
I ghosted him when I met DeceptiShawn's avatar
I had complicated feelings and didn't want Frenchy's presence to ruin his chances with me

we were only friends, but I also loved him, but also thought he'd make a terrible boyfriend
the minute I met the avatar, I cut ties; I hurt Frenchy when I thought love finally found me
but the breakup is looming, and I'm in Charlotte drinking and drunk dialing
after a 2 year silence from me, he picked up on the second ring
shit! he answered, I threw my phone to Brit; I vomited, shit
darkness...pass out...sleep
it's morning and I'm hung over; feeling better than I deserve
was I dreaming? did I call Frenchy?
my phone is ringing. shit, it's Frenchy...I'm not answering
message: "Jay, meet me...please"; 'ok' i say finally
We met somewhere public, had coffee, I was cooly coming apart at the seams
he saw me unraveling; I told him everything; his desire to kiss me was stifling
I had been so ignored lately, feeling his passion was refreshing
his eyes were pleading, but I gently refused with a smile and a 'Bye Frenchy'
I flashback to the frigid convo from the night before; I got drunk because I already knew.....

He printed out my call history; asking about 2 numbers, Isaiah's and Frenchy's
he just knew he caught me in a lie, but I had nothing to hide
DeceptiShawn showed his full face that day, but I already knew
the interrogation was a persecution, he had already decided I lied to him
he wasn't interested in my story or what I had been feeling
I learned he'd been paranoidly monitoring everything since we started dating
never finding anything, yet consistently hinting that I'm shady
meanwhile, his own antics with his ex continued; meanwhile chasing ass in VA
he spent that visit to his best friend blowing up a girl who curved him in the end
calling and texting her from the time he arrived, to a mere hour before he left
I saw the messages and immediately understood his guilt
he's an emotionally stunted mess, I'm over it, we're done here
I listened to him openly bashing me and lying to his family
claiming an imagined infidelity; disrespecting me as if he couldn't see me gathering my things
following me around to make sure I could hear the disrespect he was unabashedly
throwing at me; he disgusts me; I say nothing. I leave quietly.

My eyes are swollen and leaking, I'm not eating
breakfast and lunch are nausea and iced coffee
the world is gray, fuzzy; by day I manage to blindly autopilot
I do more crying than sleeping at night
I remember hunger pains and torrential rain
I wanted to eat badly, but the food would get in front of me and instantly disgust me
the metaphor was astounding
what I was feeling about food was the same way I felt about him
grieving the mirage of a man I fell for; loathing who he turned out to be in the end
I loved a transformer, a DeceptiShawn

his confidence a facade; in reality, egotistical, prideful and broken
I didn't know I was a healer; I was patient and encouraging
he suffocated my spark; left me in the dark of the moon
praying for the age of extinction of this pain and revenge of my fallen, broken heart
my last knight was no knight at all; a coward, a DeceptiShawn
he was never the mask I loved; misguided and emotionally retarded
he blamed me for his emotional shortcomings; projected them onto me
he was more of a paranoid robot & less of a man
I was more feeling than flesh; he turned to metal, I wrecked
I rebuilt with cold hard steel; my heartbeat sounds like bells ringing
my heart now matches my resolve; made of pure steel
it beats, but unyieldingly; it beats, but impenetrably;
it beats, but since DeceptiShawn, it rings with a steel-reverberating GONG
love has lost its meaning; yet I remain more woman than machine
more Goddess than Queen; I transformed into something amazingly frightening
a fleshy, analytical, logically-thinking,
empathic, deceptively-distant, unfeeling,
mercurial, jovial, melancholy-juggling,
friend-attracting, romance-avoiding,
equally disarming, unassuming, & intimidating,
nurturing, seeing, unyielding Goddess masquerading as a quiet Queen
I am the personality personified when fire meets ice
arctic fox meets phoenix; lava meets lightning; tornado meets Te Ka
Only now, there are in-betweens, I'm constantly evolving, ever-transforming
I am Untitled #7: Optimus Jay Ascending

"I write poetry that publishes pain from days long past, about pain that still has enough wing span to reach me and temporarily incapacitate me. I've shed enough tears to drown my own soul, my heart sometimes feels like a sinkhole. Thank the heavens for this blessed pen. It's the sword I use to slay my dragons, it's why ink and emotion seep out when I weep. This blessed pen assumes my scars and is why my open wounds don't bleed, and instead, ooze poetry."

-Jay Fisher

M(eye) Melancholy Melodic

I'm lost in a melody I can't describe
but keep hidden behind my eyes
I hear it all the time
except it magnifies when I cry
my cries, silent as a butterfly's sigh
yet still, you could define
tumultuous emotions wrecking my insides
the pain was branded on my eyes
this I knew
I cast down my glance
so my eyes wouldn't reveal the truth
I knew if I looked you in the eyes
my lips would try to lie
and should the truth be exposed
I'd lose the fight against my tears
and that somber melody would flood my ears
fearing you'd overhear
what's been hidden for years
fearing you'd see my tears and overhear
what's plagued my mind
that I've tried to hide
all these years

The Proof Is In The Sorrow

Proof that parting is nothing but sorrow
the weight in my gate forbade me to follow
drowning in misery, feeling so shallow
the pep in my step said my spirit was hollow
proof that absence makes the heart grow stronger
the hole in my soul says it can't be truer
the pain in my veins says my heart's a goner
but the choke in my throat forbids me to scream
The proof is in the sorrow
I'm trapped in an unseeable prison
I'm guilty of unseeable, unspeakable crimes
I'm completely free, and totally confined
I'm gripping reality, white knuckling
Slowly slipping, losing my mind
truth or a clever rhyme?
The proof is in the sorrow
In the land of the red puffy eyes
where tears reside at constant high tide
It's me, I'm where all sorrow resides
I curse the dam as the flood waters rise
knowing the irony of fate's design
the flood will be the dam's demise
this sorrow will be mine
the proof is in the sorrow

Safe

lock the door, lock the safe
keep me close, keep me safe
I'm on the line, neither out nor safe
you're home base, but you're not safe
with no home base, nowhere is safe
no boundaries now, what's out, what's safe?

The Same Opposite Story

My cat was alive
my doggy was too
the story was old
the house was new
the bedroom was cold
he was too
I said I was happy
it wasn't true
the notion was old
the love was new
we moved too fast
he knew it too
insecurities grew
contempt did too
the love engulfed me
suffocated me too
his past was traumatic
mine was too
him, absent dad
me, #MeToo
him, so angry
me, also true
toxic mother for me, #HerToo
emotionally unavailable and untrusting for you
me, heartbroken
you, no more glue
never again, for me
no sequel for you
moved on, says me
holding on, says you
emotions shot, for me
still a lot, for you
you feel love for me
I feel sad for you
I feel love for me
can't reach my love for you

Believer Pass To Happy

Here's a tale of a heart stolen
a heart swollen, a heart broken
of love at first sight, of soulmate's delight
of following your gut, and love's awful luck
the hardest lesson of love, you see
is that love loves nobody
and even for as happy as he made me
tis the way of love
that he also broke me
he left me a soul devoid of flesh
call me nobody
I possess trust for nobody, soul or no
with the exception of the two souls
who shared their bodies to build mine,
I have nobody
I am nobody who has nobody
possessing neither a shoulder
to lend or lean on
I'm stuck on
finding happy
Where's my happy?
he took my security
why shouldn't I at least
keep my happy?
he gave away his fidelity
why shouldn't he have my misery?
he traded loyalty for dishonesty
why can't I trade
love for sanity?
sanity is not happy
but I certainly believe
sanity is the believer's pass
to happy

HeartBrakes

Protect your heart
Run if you need to
I won't judge you
Push me away if it's what you need
Anything to prevent your heart from re-breaking
If my kisses were glue
I'd reassemble you
Do what you have to do
My heart sounds like bags of broken glass when it beats
Nevertheless, it deserves protecting
All you did was sharpen
The already piercing shards
The sharper with which to cut me
At every stuttered heartbeat
If protecting your heart
Means others must suffer
Lace your Nikes and beat it
I don't need it
Love means nothing
Respect is everything
I love you but…
Want nothing to do with you
Protect your heart
I will too
I will miss you
And wish you well
But know, my heart brakes for you
The flatline will read 'Fuhk You'.

A Mask of Your Own Face

I'm hiding in plain sight
just beneath every smile that never quite reaches your eyes
I am the sorrow that leaves you sleepless and breathless
I ripped your heart from your chest
I laughed to the beats of your last breaths
I'm not death
I'm the silence that screams in the deep of night
when the bed's too empty
and the comforter offers no comfort of sleeping tight
yearning to feel the security
of when he was there and everything was whole
I am the hole your soul fell into
in the absence of love and the presence of a lonely solitude
that dampens even the brightest of moods
and sours the sweetest of attitudes
I am a genius, smiling happily back at you
as you stare at my misery without a clue
blissfully mistaking it for happiness
blatantly missing the destruction peering out at you
from behind eyes who have cried enough tears
to fill an olympic sized swimming pool
I am your best kept secret, no one gets to see me
yet they see me everyday and fail to recognize me
I am a mask made of your own face
when you put your best face forward
I laugh thinking they actually believe it's you
and to think, they can't see me
obviously and secretly killing you

Melanin Permission Slip

Hmmm,
Brown skin and curly hair
Intriguing
Black? Latina? Native American?
All three?
Maybe, but surely too pretty to be black
And not mixed with something
Oh.
Does that make it more acceptable to love me?
Do you now have permission with the assumed dilution of my melanin?
Could your compliment be any more insulting?
This country's history is so effed up
To a degree, intelligently, I know it's a strong possibility
That there's some degree of massuh's blood
Mixed in with the motherland and native american
These are the women they raped
When they stole the country
But assuming my beauty cannot be mine
Without another race 'enhancing' me
Is curiously insulting
As if a darker version of me
Would be any less pretty…
I hear it all the time
"Oooh, giiiirl, that hair is pretty
you must have some indian in your family"
Just stop it, PLEASE
I've never looked at a beautiful woman of another race and said
'Oh, such beauty, you must have some African American in your family'
It's cringe-worthy
Why is my pretty dependent on
How far I've fallen from the African tree
Why am I pretty-dependent
Everything hinging on how you see yourself
Versus whatever you think you see in me
And whoever you voted for during this last race for Presidency
Allow me to reintroduce myself
I am soft-spoken and well mannered
I enjoy the art of using vocabulary to create poetry
I am college-educated, independent,

And somewhat spanish-speaking
I dance Kizomba, Bachata, Merengue, Salsa
And also Electric slide, Dutty Wine, and occasionally do the Wobble at family gatherings
I am black, but my skin is brown
My color is an attribute of my body, of me
Culturally, it certainly helped shape my personality and upbringing
But DOES NOT give you leave to discriminate against me
My blackness both does, but also does not, DEFINE ME
Matter of fact, it's I who should be demanding
A melanin permission slip to love me
Do you have clearance? Are you even worthy?
I am an individual who happens to be black
I am an individual
I stand before you black as ice is cold
I can trace pieces of my origin to Horntown, Virginia
Where my paternal great great great grandad
Was sold
But look at me
My curls are too defined, my attitude too optimistic
My manners too refined, my words to articulate
Your inherently racist way of thinking
Inhibits you from seeing that I'm merely you
With an enormous stigma attached to my race's identity
The reality…
My descendants were Queens and Kings who came over as cargo
mistreated, raped, beat into slavery, then sold
Their blood built this country
It stains and curses the land we're standing in
They died if they didn't do as they were told
More reality….
Today we are still being bought and sold
Still raped, murdered, mistreated, and beaten
Still the favorite feature in the police brutality videos
They're still lighting up torches and wearing white hoods
But we will persist, just as our stolen ancestors did before us
When you see this beautiful melanin
You are seeing the epitome of natural beauty
In all its glorious rebellious persistence.
Three words
I. Miss. Obama.
oh, you Blackity-Black I see
Is it still okay to love me?
Do you have clearance? Are you even worthy?

A Letter From Windy

The color has drained from the leaves
Yet still, they cling to the tree
If the tree is to survive at all
They all must fall, to make way for green
Afterall
No one has ever seen dead leaves
Sustain a growing
The hard times are dead leaves
If you let them
Those few leaves
Will either starve or poison your whole beautiful tree
The judgements will pour like rain
Do not sweat the wet
It will only feed your strength
And eventually
Make you green again
Let the whispers and gossip
Blow on me
Then use me to cleans your tree
To sever those toxic, hindering leaves
Do not let one dead leaf
Wilt and spoil your entire tree
Eventually, you will be free
And once you are
Like a bird, be ever-preening
Keep those shiny green leaves gleaming
Drop the dead leaves
And keep growing
Signed,
Windy
The Breeze

One Untitled

the art of noise
hearing is feeling
melody is the cure
to a restless soul
music is emotion
heart-breaking and soul-shaking
tension-releasing and mind provoking
it's inspiring
hearing is experiencing
music is memories
remind me
where my first kiss was
first time losing love
poetry is my sanity
it floods my veins
massages my brain
it's my anti-depressant
it's soothing
music is art is poetry
travels through me
flows from me
related like family
music is art is poetry is me

Lake Hefner, OKC 4/3/19

I cry to the wind and sea
when needing security and free vulnerability
or simply fleeing insecurity
no one listens when they speak
they can't betray me
were I a bird, I'd take to the sky
the sea caressing my belly as I fly
I'd sing my sorrow to the tide
flying until my lows rise to highs
my heart spills forth like erupting volcanoes
my brain a consistent swing between
torrential rains and tornadoes
constant screaming contests between
my horns and my halos
leaving me weathering constant storms
seeing neither an end nor a rainbow
so I cry to the wind and sea
they would never betray me
when I speak
I become both wind and sea
screaming and howling
rolling and thrashing
whispering and whistling
unforgiving and crashing
my pen gliding gently and silently
as I unleash unholy hell
on the emotions ripping through me
when i speak
my pen becomes
both whistling wind and rolling sea
I can raise as much hell as I want
and no one will hear me

342

I am a poet, melanated
my strong feminine personality
has me accidentally
emasculating these pussies
that daintily clutch their pearls
as they judge me
for being unapologetically me
only, calling them pussies
is far too complimentary
for such a strong resilient
life-creating
piece of anatomy
unless we're talking kittens
yes, these judgers are pussies
as in kitties
parading and peacocking
barking the loudest
but secretly sensitive
as a pair of PMS titties
I get it, I'm 5 foot nothing
petite and pretty
everything I say
should be gentle and placating
understand this
sometimes I'm dainty and sweet
sometimes my tongue is sharp and quick
sometimes I'm understanding
other times you can suck
this big, metaphorical lady-penis
I do what I want
and your judgement
determines nothing
about what I think of me
the clock reads 3:42am
but weather awake or sleeping
no matter what time the clock reads
its always 'mind ya own damn business' o'clock
I do what I want
I am unapologetically me

Kinda, Sorta

I have an itch, a craving
that slap my ass hard, make it sing, kind of thing
that growl, pull my hair, swear aloud, type of thing
turn my name into a prayer and a praise, sort of thing
scream it loud, make the neighbors come complain, type of thing
that ooh, it's so good, you bought a ring, kind of thing
that wet dream as you daydream about me, sort of thing
that arch my back and release everything, type of thing
that never in my wildest, wettest dreams, kind of thing
that fuhk me hard, then whisper 'sweet dreams', type of thing
that come until there's nothing left of me, kind of thing
that sex-induced, asleep immediately, sort of thing
feather kisses and massages until you dream, kind of thing
adore him while he sleeps, watch him dream, type of thing
that smiling to myself, my love is King, kind of thing
that whenever you want it, it's all yours, type of thing
that we're free, but you belong to me, sort of thing
that ask for Yoni by her name, kind of thing
It never goes away, that itch, that craving
always a him and me, kind of thing
from now, until the end of history, sort of thing
I have an itch, a craving

A Letter To My Collective Exes

I wish there was a way to speak to you without having to use words. I wish I could tolerate being in your presence long enough to know that you are well. I think of you reluctantly and very seldom allow much attention to be paid to these thoughts. You are toxic for me, but the love will always remain, and a part of me is always going to yearn for the knowledge that you are alive and well. I wish I could fully commit to not caring, but it simply is not true. However, please understand who is talking to you. I am not the broken-hearted Jay that made life amazing and miserable for you. I am a Jay no longer in love with you. I am a Jay detached from those intense feelings that used to cripple me. I no longer entertain the happy memories, I entertain no 'what-ifs'. I know definitively that fate made no mistakes in showing me you are not my soulmate. My heart does not belong to you. Certain portions may never be the same, but you occupy only what I cannot physically rid myself of. True love always leaves permanent scars, I know I cannot change this. But, I am Jay renewed, a Jay who knows better than to try to love you for a round 2. You were my dream, my fairytale. You were an epiphany, a massive coronary, a misery. You killed me, however, you also taught me that love's capabilities extend far beyond simply loving and hating. I no longer reside on that famous, ambiguous line, daring neither to love or hate too close to one side. I am now nobly-seated and meditating in a pool of peace and indifference. I love you without the urge to show you. I love you, but it doesn't consume anything else I might be thinking. I accept my love for you like I accept any other flaws I possess.

Sincerely Indifferent,

Jay

Two Untitled

I want the freedom of hopping on a plane
and making a living wherever I land
I want my structure to have no barriers
I want neither ceilings nor boundaries
I want a glass staircase to the sky
tripping over shooting stars
Orion's belt around my waist
holding my holster of happy in place
Ten paces then shoot, my joy shot clear through you
let inspiration be my wings
the breeze my only tethering
let me soar
A griffin stretching her claws and flexing her wings
hear me roar
you can't step on my happy from beneath me
only dream of reaching me
as you sleep in your gravity-ridden reality
I'm free
I can't wait on you to be weightless with me
patience is too constricting, squeezing my faith
left out of me
it isn't right
your insecurities ate holes through your flight shoes
I won't let them eat mine too
I can't wait for you
my happy floats too lightly to be weighted down with the blues
I don't need you, I need me
I want, I crave, I believe,
I need, I am, I love
Free

Savage Meets Reality

I approach love intelligently
I rationally consult my common sense
to sense what is and what isn't
Love is an empty word in and of itself
comprised and concocted from misconceptions,
from each person's no-account accounts
of what really happened
and how it could have been prevented
of why it didn't last
of how the passion burned out with Christmas past
and the side chick he slept with was a downgrade
but you stuck with him because he deserves a bad bitch…
Love has no logic
they share two letters and nothing else
we claim it and aim it at our fears
allowing it to give us reason to do
the opposite of what we know to be
the right thing to do
does he really deserve a 'bad bitch'
or are you afraid that you deserve better?
now you're a self-proclaimed savage
sitting in a pumpkin patch
slaying nothing but bum-kins that no one else wants
because after you took him back
he realized he could do better
and wanted a woman who wanted better for herself…
you think you're playing the field now?
you're sifting through the dump
slaying garbage
slaying nothing

Frenchy Explained - 11/4/16

I don't understand Frenchy. The connection we have is astoundingly simple in that way. No matter where life takes us, no matter how angry I get, no matter how many times I send him away, he always comes back. We always find ourselves sitting in the same room, reaffirming what we don't understand; which is us and whatever we are; reaffirming this bond. You see, we have never belonged to each other. Time separates us time and time again. Yet when we see each other again, it's like the timeline was never broken. Frenchy thinks he knows me better than anybody. I don't completely agree, but he's also not wrong. His understanding of me is simplistic, but he also seems to understand me deeply and psychologically simultaneously. What others see, all the mind-bending complexities that make me, well me, he makes easy sense from the hieroglyphics. He is one of few humans where, in his eyes, I'm simple. He doesn't bother to question what makes me the way I am, he just accepts it...easily. 'That's just Fish'. He gets it. I wrote this poem (referring to "Frenchy's Watching") while watching him read another poem loosely inspired by him (referring to "Excuse My English"). For me, it personifies our simple acceptance of each other, and our fear of belonging to each other. You will never hear me say I want to belong to Frenchy. You won't hear him say the reverse either. Collectively, we hate shackles. But, when we are in the same room, the air is heavy; heavy with all the things we do not and dare not say. We stare, we smile, we think, but no, we won't speak about certain things; even though we know we can tell each other anything. Romance and it's silly notions and ideas make us flighty. I don't want to be with him, nor him with me; yet somehow, I still belong to him, and he belongs to me, but freely. Sometimes my emotions get the best of me and I can't help thinking how it would be, but I only think, never speak. In the end, I always end up smiling. I wouldn't change a thing, but sometimes, I smile wondering what he could be thinking. I think he smiles sometimes for the very same reasons. Sometimes he smiles at me as if he can see me considering the thing that we don't talk about considering...Grace.

Myself Talking To Me

I deserve to be valued
I'm dependable and always there and you,
Well
You don't deserve my loyalty
Nor is it reciprocated so from what I see
You are ungrateful and greedy
Your are energy sucking and soul-crushingly needy
BACK
THE
FUHK UP
OFF
OF
ME
I see
I 'see' you
I see through your ego's fragility
I see your insecurity
I see your vulnerabilities
I see your triggers & handicapped sign
I see your severe emotional disability
You are as wise as a puddle is deep
Twice as weak-minded as the sheep you keep
You're not even a wolf
You're a lamb dreaming of possessing wolf's teeth
You are pretending your wool is wolf hide
But when slaughter comes
No doubt, you will still be fried
You are as low as the people you step on, and even lower than the ground they piss on
You are nobody beneath that fake mountain of humility
Your mental fortitude has no girth or virility
It's flaccid and skinny
And here I am a Queen, trying to build up a worm
I dishonor my own royalty
Know your worth Queen
Myself talking to me.

Man vs. Vulnerability vs. Me

Voice of insecurity
my apologies for wanting to see the reality
I see darkness through the windows
blank stares reveal cloudy skies, dark eyes
torrential rains threaten, floods in disguise
what are you hiding?
what am I not supposed to see?
something's casting shadows, why the secrecy?
I don't belong to you, don't believe I want to
still strangers, we don't know that yet
or maybe you do, is that what scares you?
none of it is coherent is it?
feelings for her still sting, don't they?
old scars still ooze and bleed, don't they?
they appear scabbed and healed, don't they?
then knock you on your ass, don't they?
they don't own or define you, do they?
because you've moved on, haven't you?
haven't you? Aren't you sleeping at night?
do you think of her and feel lonely?
is that why your bed feels so empty,
why you get in it but don't get sleepy?
do you crave the attention of anybody
who will distract you from remembering
that when you think of her touch
it stops you from breathing?
what does this stranger do for you?
why does she keep challenging you?
why does she ask things you can't yet admit to?
is that new stranger plotting on you?
what could she possibly want from you?
she doesn't want you to save her, does she?
she's not asking to love you, is she?
she can't love again, she's not capable
is she?
she's just curious probably
there are no reasons for her interest
can you give her any?
perhaps she once loved a shut-down King...maybe

could he have left her with questions unanswered?
surely that's a tangible possibility
maybe she just wants to know what you're thinking
maybe your answers will silence some of her constant questioning
maybe her shut-down King, the former man of her dreams
behaved similarly
maybe she wants hints from the man's side of the story
why be so weary? You are not her King
I doubt she wants you to be
What threat is she posing?
is all of this because she wants to be yours?
is she trying to fix her problems by fixing yours?
are you weary unnecessarily? Maybe
Afterall,
she's just curious probably
she has no reason to be intrigued
can you give her any?

"People tend to run from two things: things that genuinely scare them, and things they want deeply and sincerely, but are afraid they don't deserve." -Jay Fisher

-paraphrased from a journal entry of mine dated 11/19/16

It would, If he

I always thought I'd end up with someone strong
a man of top intelligence and integrity
a man with discipline and dignity
a man that will live and love with me
I always thought he would find his way to me
that our love would just happen...coincidentally and suddenly
that it would seem almost heavenly
that it would feel like destiny tapping me
that it would race and stop my heart simultaneously
when he's in close proximity to me
what if he can see my growing affections
what if he looks at me and I look away
can he see right through me?
what if he can see my hopes that he
feels something for me
that I hope his search for her ends with me
I would never be able to make eye contact
without having a near heart attack
that he can see my feelings
I fear if I let him close enough to me
my eyes will become windows and betray me
what if he kisses me
and realizes that he has me
what if he knows my like for him is so intense
its discomforting
what if he knows that's why I squirm when his eyes bore into me
what if he knows his voice melts me
even worse, what if he loves me already
what if I get scared, try to flee and he doesn't let me
what if he's the one I need
what if I'm the one for him
what if his heart is pure
what if he's the cure
to my broken
would it work if he was fearless enough
for both of us
loving him scares me
what if I can't open up enough
what if he can't break through

what if my wall is too tough
what if he knows I'm trapped behind it
what if I need him to save me
what if his love penetrates the wall
what if it falls
what if he finally sees inside and hates it all
what if my lack of bravery and security
stops him from seeing his future when he looks at me
what if I'm just overthinking it all
what if the wall falls
and he loves me still
flaws and all
what if it all depends on him
what if he's the cure to my broken
what if I need him
what then
if it's meant to be
it would work
it would if he
......
Fill in this blank for me

Invisible Queen

I stand before you
You see clear through me
Your search is avid
You're looking for me
Not seeing me
Never choosing me
Can't find me
You're looking everywhere
For your happy
Looking everywhere
Except at me
Standing right before you
I am your Queen
I am royalty
I will not bow to you
I see you
I am royalty
You are just pretending
I can see you
You're one of a kind
But compassionless and blind
I see you are not awakened
I understand, but lack the patience

Positive Todaily Mantra

I woke up today
I smiled at the sun today
I turned my salt lamp on today
I lit candles today
I burned an incense today
I meditated today
I thanked my ancestors today
I exercised today
I drank water today
I made art today
I listened to music today
I greeted my plants today
I made coffee today
I danced today
I went on the patio today
I love myself today
I radiate good energy today
I wrote this today
I'm grateful,
Thank you today.

"You are not the center of my universe. I AM the center of my universe, the Queen of my own great nation which is my body. I do what I want and only because I choose to. You are allowed to be here in my Universe because I say so. I chose to have you here, but it is a gift that I will give and take as I see fit. I love you, but you do not come before my mental health and peace of mind. If you disturb my peace, peace be unto you as I chuck deuce and send you through the metaphorical moon door. Byeeeieee! Hi, My name is Jay and I'm a poetic goddess. Also, I do what I want. Your name and presence are optional...the end."
-Jay Fisher

Tears With My Coffee

Every year with this day
Every year with this grief
Every year with this journey
Every pain towards peace

Every year with these questions
Every year with these tears
Every year in her absence
Even worse when she's here

Every year scarred
Every year stunted
Every year pretending
There's a bond that means something

There's tears with my coffee
Every this day in May
There's tears in my coffee
To salvage this day

There's tears with my coffee
There's tears with my growth
Whether celebrating or grieving
There's tears with both

Tears with my coffee
To salvage this day
Tears with my coffee
Every this day in May

Water

Life
energy
cosmic flow
water is
the soul of existence
moon is maestro
gravity is the song
the push and pull
moves the tides
tide is lead
our emotions, the follow
see-through if shallow
if deep, you see
only your reflection
a glistening, shimmering
tangible version of the sky
soothing when slow
abrasive when rushing
beautiful, comforting
terrifying, deadly
water is what it means
to be a woman

Roses Are Mean

I no longer believe in the notion of love, or that people deserve the benefit of the doubt. Second chances are hardly needed for those already deserving, those who know what it means to cherish. You aren't worthy, and you are well aware. I am a delicate rose with thorns on my tongue. Wear gloves before speaking or picking me. These thorns can become kitten mittens just as quickly as they can turn deadly. Ten cuidado. I do not dilute my honesty and if that's too sour for your cup of tea, I'm sure Kermit can get you a dose of courage from Miss Piggy, you know, in case you need some help confronting me, #SipsTea. Don't expect me to tiptoe around your assholery, as if you didn't get the memo when you met me. Who the FUHK do you think i am? I am a poetic sagittarian dream with sharp words and a curvy body. I am Nefertiti sharing my crown with the rest of my beautiful black Queens. We make this shit look easy, but trust me, this fuhking crown is heavy. My vivacious royalty will not be singed or subdued by the likes of little-dick energy or any human lacking vaginal fortitude. If that sounds too confusing, too challenging, or too aggressive for you, I am absolutely the wrong rose for you. My rose is delicate to a soft hand. You won't feel the thorns unless you force it. Before you go claiming roses are mean, check your own energy.

Yoni-Vee

puppet master extreme
no matter how angry, emotional, or mean
I keep you saying anything
to get back into me
truth? well, depends on who's talking
you'll bend reality to look like me
bent and enticing
just to keep me bending over
with you anxiously behind me
I distort perceptions and shatter moral compasses
all in the name of tasting bliss
all for a succulent slice of this
from my lips have whispered the sweet words of war
I've brought entire empires to their knees
I am Yoni-Vee
your source, your power, your weakness, your truth
mind control is real
I'm the proof
it amazes even me at what
a human can be enticed to do
at my hands, they become cannibals; addicts
fleshy, dangly appendages become bricks
they drop to their knees before me
nuzzling my panties; silently revering me
the mere scent of me
causing an uncontrollable need to feed
to bury your face in me
and sigh deeply
I am your solace, your escape, your serenity
I remove you from a world of pressure
and swaddle you in the moist warmth
of my nurturing femininity
I am key to your sanity and mental clarity
I am Yoni-Vee
I ground you, my walls hold your legacy
you retain your connection to the earth
through me
I am Goddess of life and pleasure
my lips, the gates to your inner peace

I am protector of your masculine energy
nurturer of your emotional well-being
I am the connection to your creation
the link to and creator of all humanity
have a need for warmth, grounding, a snack, or clarity?
cum see me
I am Yoni-Vee

Word Association, Because Writer's Block is REAL

Gimme a word
verb, rhymes with herb
who's idea was it to spell that with an 'h'?
lightbulb, genius, dummy
don't go political, LOL
but be polite
pilot, flight deck, flood lights, India Aerie
curry, masala, rice, basmati
maserati
why does my brain always want to rhyme?
melon rind
jubblies, AD, singing, missing
nothing, free, flying
little blue and black birdie
the sky, she died, bye best friend
childhood ends
early trauma, toxic mama
escape, saving grace, My Daddy
happy, peace, healing, surgery
knees, daughter mom, gone, empty
Cousin Pete, grief, cherished memories
laughter, loyalty, Chris Brown, Deuces
Exes, stay woke, ninja's creepin
TLC, alphabet soup, vocabulary
poetry, hiding, scary, vulnerability
Brené Brown, doo-doo brown
poop, litterbox, Kitten-formerly-known-as-Prince
clingy, squeaking, sweet
yummy, coffee, morning, awakening
sun, fix, phoenix, soldier
frozen solid, impenetrable, The Wall
Game of Thrones, King, Jamie, Cersie
incest, nasty, nekkit white booties
bologna, sammich, sexuals,
WHAT ARE THOSE
jesus sandals, leave room for Jesus
social distancing, Covid-19, quarantitty
Sanity, fresh air, nature
STOP CUTTING DOWN THE TREES

mother earth dying, humans suck
lollipop, candy, cavities
teeth, bite me, puppy, teething
snaggletooth, gap, jeans, Ginuwine
Dream & Story, weird kid names
baby goats, tiny psychos
looney bin, crazy, glue, art, painting
brush, hair, locs, journey
new growth, self-acceptance
body and hair confidence
Black Girl Magic
unsung, voices, lullaby, baby
sleep, bed, floor, carpet, green
plants, windosil, bird watching
beauty, trees, wind and leaves
a piece of me is missing
void, droid, Star Wars, non-violent
Martin, funny, comedy, Kevin Hart
IG, social media, popularity contests
trolling, bullying, police brutality
I can't breathe, Say their names
keep fighting
temptation, snack, 'yasss hunny'
rainbows, Rupaul, "You better werk", PRIDE
love is love, stronger together
unity, love, peace, free

Acknowledgments

Believe it or not, writing this section is the hardest part for me. My first and biggest shot-out is to my Papa Bear, because he is my most favorite human walking this earth. This book also goes out to the humans that love me, to the humans that support me, to the humans that build me up, to the humans that fill my cup, to the humans that make me feel at peace, to the humans I love and can't wait to squeeze, to my fellow beautiful black queens, to my royal and regal black kings, to people of color and our allies, to defying the odds and being loud, to making noise and taking up space, to standing up for humanity, to keeping each other safe. This book goes out to women, men, and all of the in-betweens that society keeps trying to pretend not to see. I see you. And even though this particular book isn't kid-friendly, this one is for our babies, may we encourage them to follow their dreams with a reckless abandon like nothing the world has ever seen. This one is for my family. I guess I should have warned them in the beginning about some of the poems they may find appalling (insert cover my eyes emoji). This one is for freedom of speech and being nothing less than who you truly are. This one is for being unapologetically you, for being comfortable and basking in the skin you were born in. Shot out to my fellow Intuitive Planning team members and my humans in the dance scene. We will make it through this time of limited hugs and quality time (insert crying emoji). Shot out to my dance frat, Fraternity MPK #squaaad. Shot out to my melanin. And as always, even though Covid is out here killing dreams and cockblocking, never stop loving; never stop dancing. I wish you peace and positive manifestations. <3